ALL I NEED IS LOVE

A Play For Teens

BY

KATHLEEN MORRIS

Rouge Publishing

978-1-927828-24-3

This book is a work of fiction. Names, characters, places, and incidences are the product of the author's imagination or are used fictitiously. Any resemblance to actual events, locals, or person, living or dead, is coincidental.

Rouge Publishing

ISBN 978-1-927828-24-3

OTHER BOOKS BY KATHLEEN MORRIS

Deep Bay Series

Deep Bay Vengeance

Deep Bay Relic

Deep Bay Legacy (Coming 2014)

Blood War Series

The Prion Attachment

Blood Purge (Coming 2014)

Short Inspirations Series

Size Seven Shorts

Short End Of The Stick

Shortcut To Alaska

Short Stories

Along The Way - 12 Short Stories You Can Read Along The Way

Plays

Time Will Tell - An Easter Play

Even Me - A Christmas Play For Your Sunday School

All I Need Is Love - A Play For Teens

Lost And Found - A Children's Christmas Play

Gotta Love It - A Humorous Play About Rural Life

How - To Books

How To Make Eye Catching Ebook Covers Easily

Available on Amazon.com

A NOTE FROM THE AUTHOR

This is a serious play about drug abuse among young people. With a cast of six, and one scene throughout this one act play, two sisters fight for their parents love. Without it, one of the sisters turns to drugs to find the love that she is looking for. This play could be used as a wonderful teaching tool for both parents and kids alike.

It was written as a college assignment in 2002 and performed to educate and explore some of the reasons behind drug abuse. It is my hearts cry, and my hope for all God's creatures, to love each other properly, so we don't lose even one precious soul to the painful addictions that plague this world.

Table of Contents

A Note From The Author 7
Characters 9
Scene One 11
At rise of curtain 11
ABOUT THE AUTHOR 29

CHARACTERS

Mom:

A very controlling mean strict person.

Fred:

He is the dad. Easy-going. A wimp.

Jackie:

The oldest daughter…about fifteen.

Karen:

The younger daughter…ten years old.

Mojo:

Bad influential friend.

Kitty:

Mojo's sidekick…another bad influential friend.

SCENE ONE

The living room of Jackie and Karen's home. It is just after school and Jackie has invited her new friends Mojo and Kitty to come over for a while.

AT RISE OF CURTAIN

Jackie, dressed in the latest fashions, opens the door into the living room of her spotless home. Expensive trinkets are placed meticulously in order or on the glass shelves and coffee table. Mojo and Kitty obviously kids from the wrong side of the tracks, follow her. Mojo is sucking on a sucker and wearing dark glasses, a backwards baseball cap, and a big t-shirt with the ends not tucked into his pants. He walks with an exaggerated "cool" stride. Kitty, chewing gum wildly, dressed and walking the same as Mojo, hangs on his arm, and appears to be the brainier part of the defective duo. Karen, dresses just as well as her sister, follows the bunch through the door into the living room and closes it.

Jackie:

Well this is it. (*Pointing her way into the door as a way to welcome her guests in*)

Mojo:

(*Looking around in wonder*) Yo Man!... This place rocks! (*He lets go of Kitty's arm and walks around looking extensively at everything*)

Kitty:

(*Walks around and looks at everything too*) Wow...What are you guys rich or something? (*She touches everything and then stopped to pick up a very expensive vase*)

Jackie:

We're not rich…(*She says this defensively as if she were ashamed*)...and DON'T

TOUCH THAT! (*She pulls the vase out of Kitty's hand and gently places it back in its original spot*)

Kitty:
(*Kitty rolls her eyes and clicks her tongue in a snobby way*) Looks like it to me. (*She continues to look around the room with Mojo opening cupboards and snooping*)

Karen:
We're rich! (*looks at Jackie funny*) Aren't we Jackie! (*Said as a statement rather than a question*)

Jackie:
(*Jackie looks at Karen with embarrassment*) Karen...SHUT UP! (*She's annoyed at her sister's juvenile antics*)

Karen:
Don't tell me to shut up!

Jackie:
I can tell you to shut up if I want to!

Karen:

Yah right!

Jackie:

YAH RIGHT! (*Says this more as a matter of fact tone and very much louder than her sister*) NOW GET LOST!

Karen:

NO! (*Argues this snappy and quick with defiant arms crossed, shrugging and looking away*)

(*Mojo and Kitty have suddenly stopped their snooping and become aware and annoyed at the arguing*)

Mojo,

Would you guys chill out man…you're bummin' the Mojo. (*Says this slowly with a spaced out tone*)

Kitty:

(Strides over to Mojo) Maybe they need the Mojo's L...O...V...E potion. (*They wink at each other*)

Mojo:

You know it babe...You know it! (*Mojo clowns around doing some kind of a jig, hi-fives Kitty, and blows on his hand and shakes it*) Whoa, I'm good. (*Reaches in pocket for something. Can't find it. Pulls out everything but what he's looking for. Tries other pocket, pulls out paper, pens, odd things...and looks at it*)

Karen:

What's *love* potion?

(*Mojo and Kitty snicker and Jackie glares at them*)

Jackie:

Never mind Karen…you don't want to know. (*Says this in a protective tone*)

Karen:

Yes I do! (*She glares at Jackie with rage*)

Kitty:

You never heard of LOVE potion? (*Both Mojo and Kitty snicker again*) Honey child...Where *have* you been? (*She says this as a statement more than a question and draws out the word "have" as she says it mockingly*)

Jackie:

Leave her alone, she's only ten!

(*Karen cranks her head around to Jackie and gives her a dirty look, then she turns back to Mojo and looks interested in what he is rummaging around in his pocket to find*)

Mojo:

(*Mojo stops looking in his pocket for a minute*) Sweet *thang*....love potion is the *Mojo candy*...

Karen:

(*Karen looks puzzled at every word Mojo is saying*) Hugh?

Mojo:

You know...(*He twists his face up like he can't believe she doesn't know*)...Easy "*e*"?

Karen:

I still don't get it. (*Puzzled with hands out and palms up*)

Kitty:

Daaaa (*snorts and rolls her eyes*) It's called *Ecstasy...*

Karen:

I knew that.

Jackie:

Karen!!! (*Scolds her like a disappointed mother would*)

Karen:

What?...(*Looks at Jackie with an evil eye*)...You don't know everything about me Jackie.

Mojo:

All right...I knew it was in here somewhere. (*Pulls out a bottle of pills from his pocket*) Here...try some. (*He gives the whole bottle of pills to Karen*)

Jackie:

(*Angrily pulls it from Karen's hand*) Don't give her that!...I told you we're not into that.

Karen:

Give it back... I want to try it!

Jackie:

No...*you don't!*

Karen:

Yes I do!

(*Mojo and Kitty stand there laughing and cheering the sisters on as they continue to fight for the pills. Jackie stuffs the bottle into her pocket and Karen continues to argue that she wants it*)

(*Suddenly, their mom and dad come in the door after a long day of work. The arguing is still going on*)

(*Enter the parents*)

Karen:
Give it!

Jackie:
No!

Mom:
What is going on here? (*Fred, the dad takes off his shoes and jacket as well as the mom*)

Karen:
Jackie's pushing me around again!

(*The girls are pushing each other*)

Jackie:
And *she* is a *brat!*

Karen:
Am not!

Jackie:
Are too!

Karen:
Bully!

Jackie:
Suck!

Mom:
Enough...That's enough!...(*She rubs her brow and cringes*) Just stop it!

Karen:
She started it! (*Pointing at Jackie*)

(*Jackie's mouth just hangs open in shock*)

Mom:
(*Mom yells*) Jackie...How many times did I tell you to act your age?

Jackie:
But Mom...

Mom:

(*Mom is still yelling*) But mom nothing...We leave you in charge and this is what you do…(*She holds up her hands with her palms out. She turns to Mojo and Kitty*)...and just who might you be? (*She looks them up and down in disgust*)

Kitty:

I'm Kitty, and this is the Mojo. (*She punches him in the arm playfully*)

Mom:

The who?

Mojo:

WHAS UP...(*Looks out of his shades and wipes his hand off holding it out to shake her hand. Mom doesn't shake*)

Mom:

Ah, um...*You're* friends? (*Mom glares in disgust at Jackie*)

Karen:

(*Says like a tattletale*) Yah, and Jackie told them they could come over.

Mom:

(*Growling and yelling again*) Jackie, I said no friends didn't I? No friends when were not home! NO FRIENDS MEANS NO FRIENDS...WHAT PART OF THAT DON'T YOU UNDERSTAND? Honestly (*She turns to Fred*) you could help you know. (*She swats him on the arm as he cringes*)

Fred:

Well dear...(*He says with a small voice*)...You don't have to get so...

Mom:

Get out...(*She commands both Mojo and Kitty*)...the both of you! (*She starts to push them now*) Jackie shouldn't have invited you over.

Jackie:

Mom...don't. (*She is embarrassed and upset*)

(*Mom continues to push Mojo and Kitty out the door. Kitty grows angry and takes the mom's hands off of her*)

Kitty:

FINE!...Like...we're out a here anyways RICH WITCH! Come on Mojo. (*She rolls her eyes and acts insulted while pulling Mojo's shirt to follow her*)

(*Mom's mouth hangs open in shock*)

Mojo:

Bummer! (*He says this slowly and exits with Kitty*)

Mom:

(*Closes door while yelling*)...And don't come back! My girls don't hang around with your kind!

Jackie:

(*Yelling. Obviously upset and crying now*) Mom...YOU HAVE COMPLETELY HUMILIATED ME IN FRONT OF MY FRIENDS. I HATE YOU!

Mom:

Friends?...You call those friends? I can't believe it. Fred...(*She looks at him for support*)...you tell her those are not the kind of friends my daughters will be associated with. Never!

Fred:

Well...I don't know...(*Slow and mouselike*)

Mom:

(*Yelling*) They are not friends! Do you hear me? We didn't bring you up like that... And we also thought we taught you how to be responsible. Think of your sister for once instead of yourself. My goodness child, do you ever listen? I said NO FRIENDS OVER WHEN WE'RE NOT HOME!

Jackie:

(*Still crying*) Not home? Mom you're never home! We never have friends over!

Mom:

(*Yelling*) What?... And that's the thanks I get? I work my butt off for you girls. Your father works his butt off...(*She nudges him*) and this is the thanks we get?

Karen:

(Sucking up) *I* love you mommy. (*She put her arms around her*)

Mom:

We give you girls everything! You wanted a new flat screen for your bedroom, you got it. You wanted a new iPhone, laptop, iPad, you got it...and you have the nerve to complain?

Jackie:

But Mom...

Mom:

But mom nothing! I didn't need this Jackie. Today of all days. I have one of my migraines again and we just lost a major deal at work. GOOD GRIEF GIRL!

Fred:

Um...I'll go run your bath for you dear. (*He shuffles around like a servant getting her things. He exits*)

Karen:

Come on mommy, I'll give you a head massage. (*Turns to give Jackie a wide smile as if to say she won*)

Mom:

Oh, you're so sweet my baby. How come your sister can't be more like you? I've given her *everything.* What else could she possibly need? (*She puts her arm around Karen's neck and they both exit the room*)

(*Jackie stands in the middle of the room all by herself in tears*)

Jackie:

(*Pulls the bottle of pills out of her pocket and looks at them as she dries her tears*) All I need...is *love.*

(*She opens the bottle of pills and swallows them all*)

THE END

ABOUT THE AUTHOR

Award-winning author Kathleen Morris has written numerous articles, poetry, and short stories published in various Saskatchewan newspapers. Her poem *Refuge* is published in a book anthology titled *A Golden Morning*. She has written many plays and skits including her play titled *Gotta Love It*, winner of Dancing Sky Theatre's rural writing contest in 2001 where it was also performed by the theatre troupe in Meacham, Saskatchewan.

Deep Bay Vengeance is Kathleen's first novel followed by its sequel *Deep Bay Relic*. She also writes non-fiction inspirational books about funny stories from her own life. Her latest novel is called *The Prion Attachment,* first book in the *Blood War Trilogy.* When she's not writing, she enjoys spending time with her husband Barry and their three grown children at her home in Saskatchewan, Canada. For more on Kathleen Morris please check out her Amazon Author page at Amazon .com.

OTHER BOOKS BY KATHLEEN MORRIS

Deep Bay Series
Deep Bay Vengeance
Deep Bay Relic
Deep Bay Legacy (Coming 2014)
Blood War Series
The Prion Attachment
Blood Purge (Coming 2014)
Short Inspirations Series
Size Seven Shorts
Short End Of The Stick
Shortcut To Alaska
Short Stories
Along The Way - 12 Short Stories You Can Read Along The Way
Plays
Time Will Tell - An Easter Play
Even Me - A Christmas Play For Your Sunday School
All I Need Is Love - A Play For Teens
Lost And Found - A Children's Christmas Play
Gotta Love It - A Humorous Play About Rural Life

How - To Books

How To Make Eye Catching Ebook Covers Easily

Available on Amazon.com

www.ingramcontent.com/pod-product-compliance
Lightning Source LLC
LaVergne TN
LVHW010108110826
845155LV00028B/551